THIS BOOK BELONGS TO:

COLOR TEST PAGE

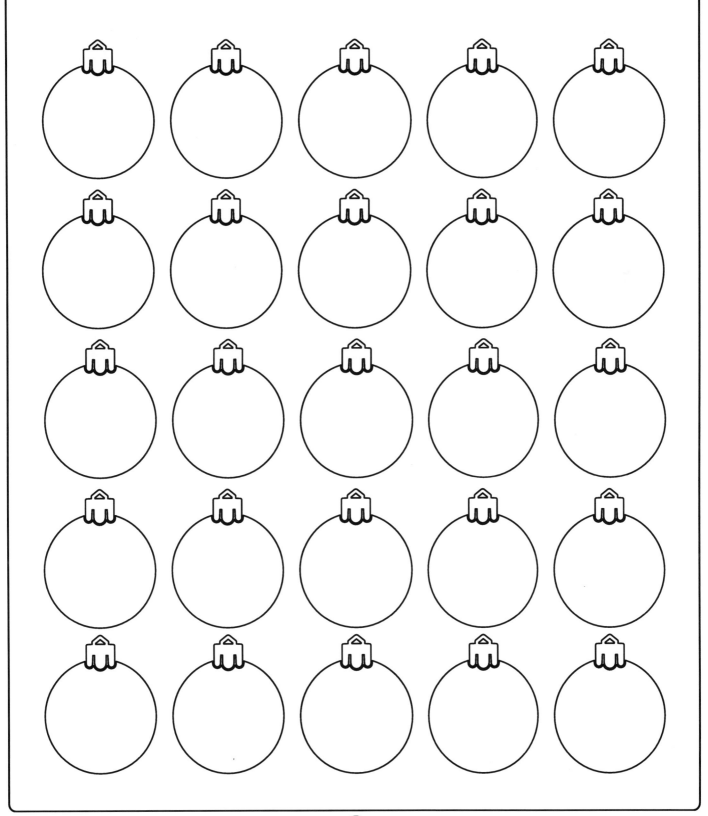

Christmas Tracing

Place the Christmas presents under the trees

Trace and Color

5

Trace the numbers

Trace the numbers

Christmas ABC

Fill in the missing letters and finish the alphabet

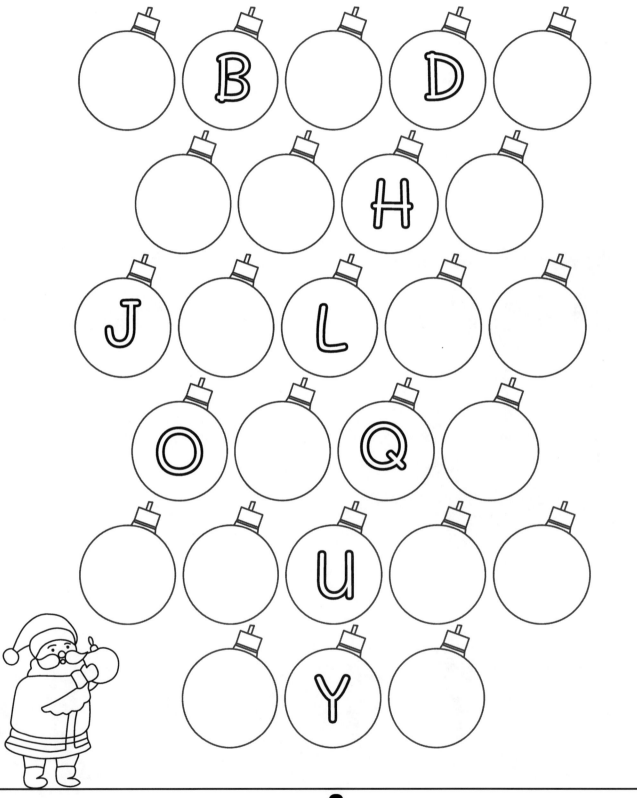

How many?

Count the winter objects and write the numbers in the box

How many Snowman do you see?

Color the Christmas tree

Find the other half

 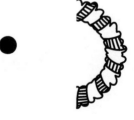

Trace the letters

a b c d e
f g h i j
k l m n o
p q r s t
u v w x y
z

Maze 1

14

Color the Christmas item that is different

Christmas decor

**Finish drawing the Christmas Tree.
Color and decorate it.**

How Many

21

I SPY Christmas Tree

22

Maze 2

23

Christmas Count

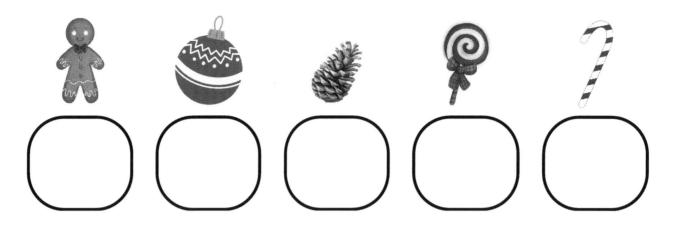

Dot Markers

25

CHRISTMAS SWEETS
Color the sweets correctly

Trace the letters to make the word:

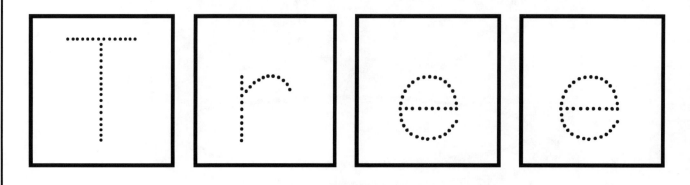

Spell the word

M N W

O S A N

Connect the dots

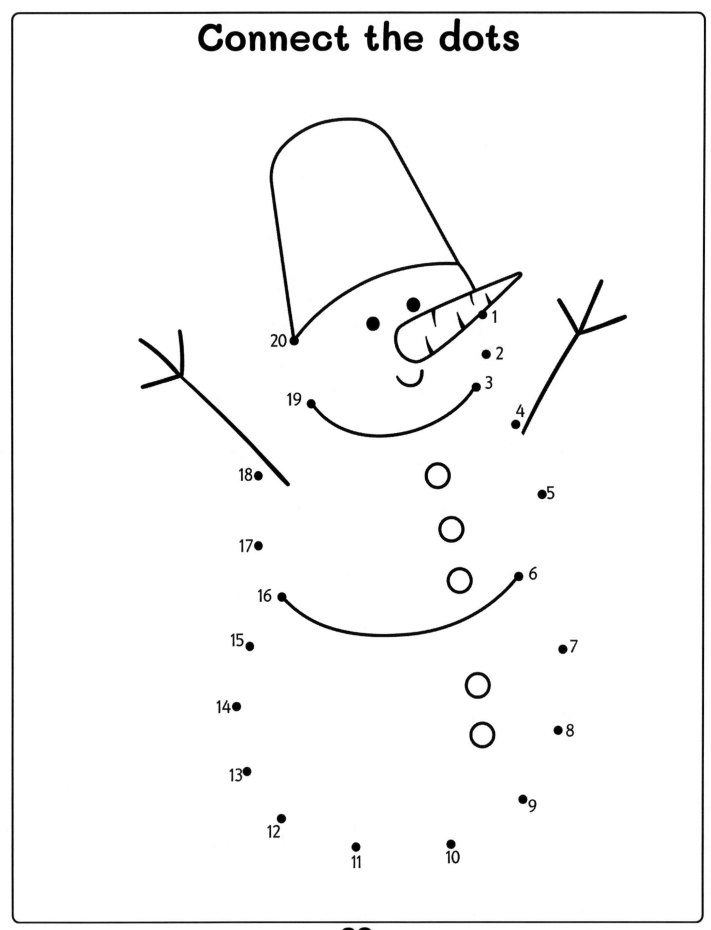

30

COUNTING CATS AND DOGS

Write the answers at the box provided below

CATS DOGS

MATCH THE NUMBER

Draw a line to match the number to its name

 •   • Seven

 •   • Five

 •   • Nine

 •   • One

 •   • Six

 •   • Four

 •   • Eight

 •   • Two

 •   • Three

Connect the dots

37

Trace the letters to make the word:

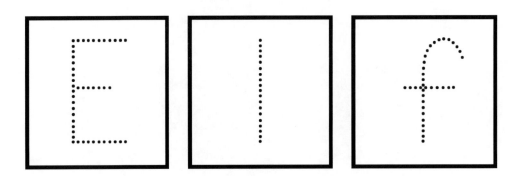

Count and write how many

5 + 3 = ☐

4 + 2 = ☐

3 + 4 = ☐

6 + 3 = ☐

7 + 0 = ☐

39

Count and write how many

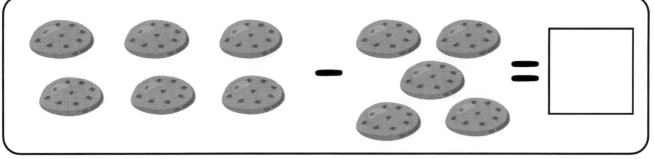

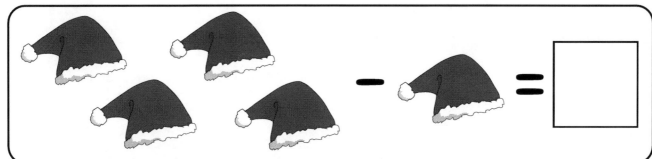

🎀🎀🎀🎀 - 4 = ☐

9 - 🧤🧤🧤🧤🧤 = ☐

Dot Markers

SKIP COUNT BY 2'S. FILL IN THE MISSING NUMBERS FOR EACH SWEATER.

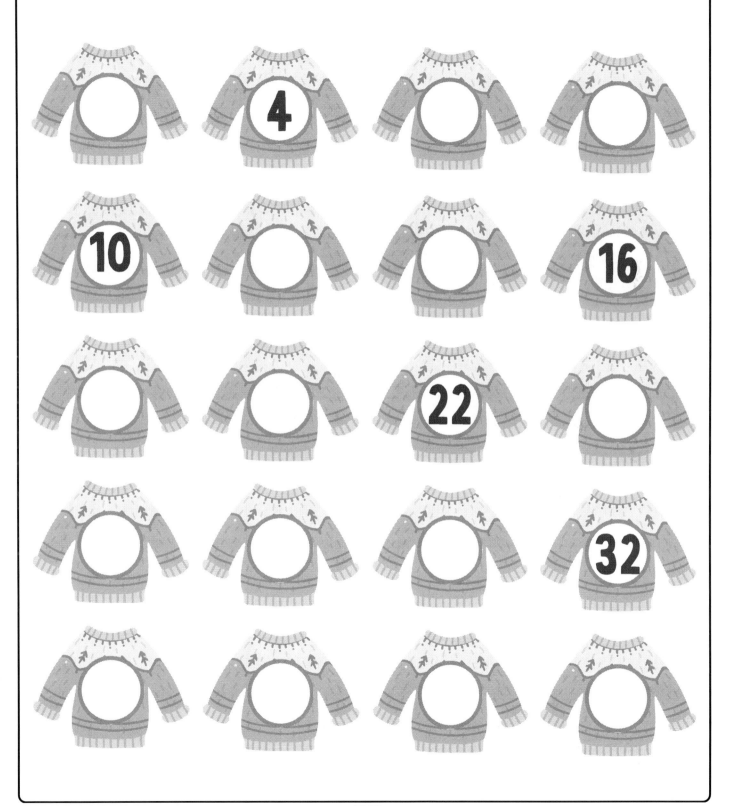

Count & Mark

Count the elements in each box and mark the correct number

Dot Markers

Trace the letters to make the word:

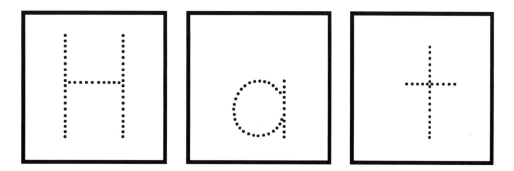

Color by Number

Color each part of the picture with the color next to each number.

How many Gingerbread do you see?

Maze 3

Dot Markers

53

Spot 5 differences and color

Count the objects and color the correct number

Connect the dots

57

Count & Color

Count and color the exact number of Christmas elements

| 2 |
| 5 |
| 3 |
| 1 |
| 6 |
| 7 |
| 4 |

Dot Markers

MERRY CHRISTMAS

Tracing Word

Angel

Tree

Ball

Holly

63

Tracing Word

Maze 4

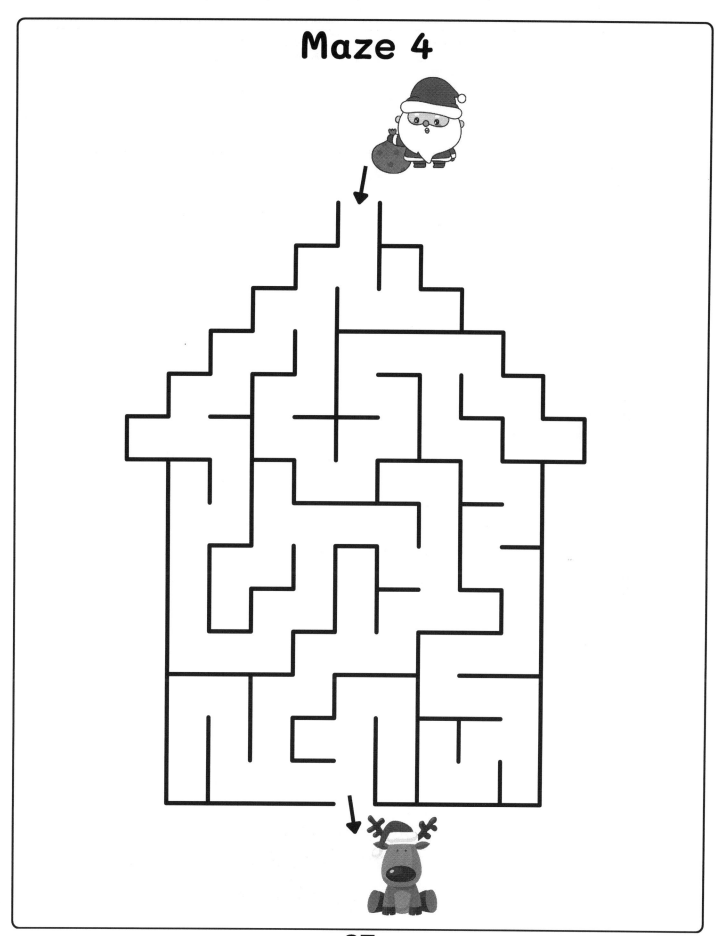

Find penguin among the snowman

66

Find the other half

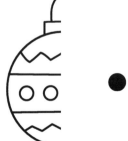
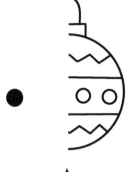
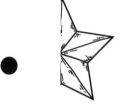
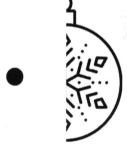

Color by Number

1. orange   2. blue   3. dark blue
4. red   5. green   6. yellow   7. brown

Trace and Color

Gingerbread

Find The Shadow

Maze 5

Colour the pictures and cross over the words

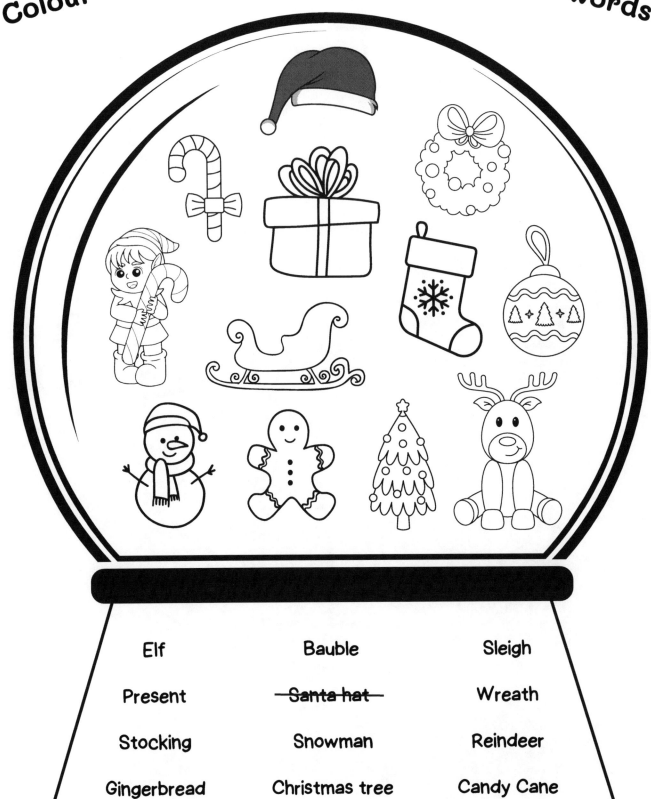

Elf	Bauble	Sleigh
Present	~~Santa hat~~	Wreath
Stocking	Snowman	Reindeer
Gingerbread	Christmas tree	Candy Cane

Connect the dots

77

Find The Shadow

Maze 6

80

FIND THE DIFFERENCE

Circle the different one between pictures

Color the snowglobe

Color by Number

Use the key at the bottom of the page to color the picture

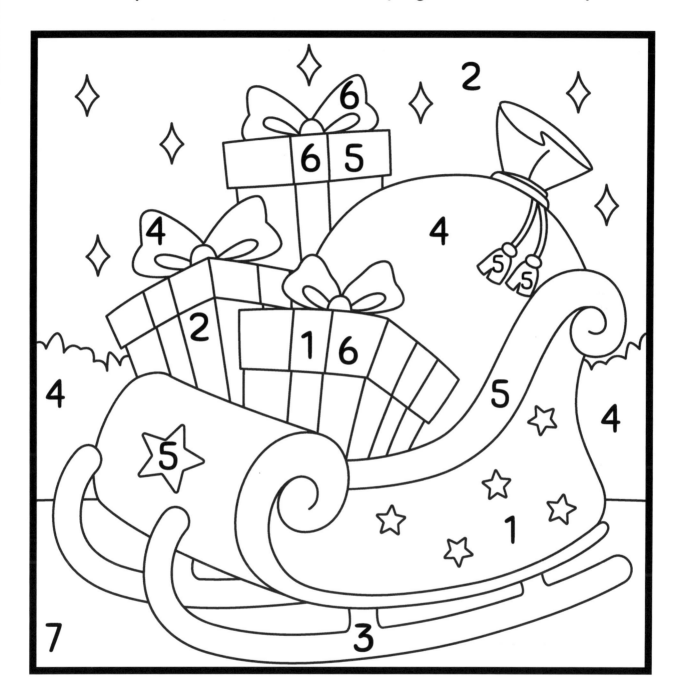

1. red 2. blue 3. brown
4. green 5. yellow 6. pink 7. gray

Maze 7

84

Christmas - What Comes Next?

Cut out the images at the bottom. Paste the image that comes next in each pattern.

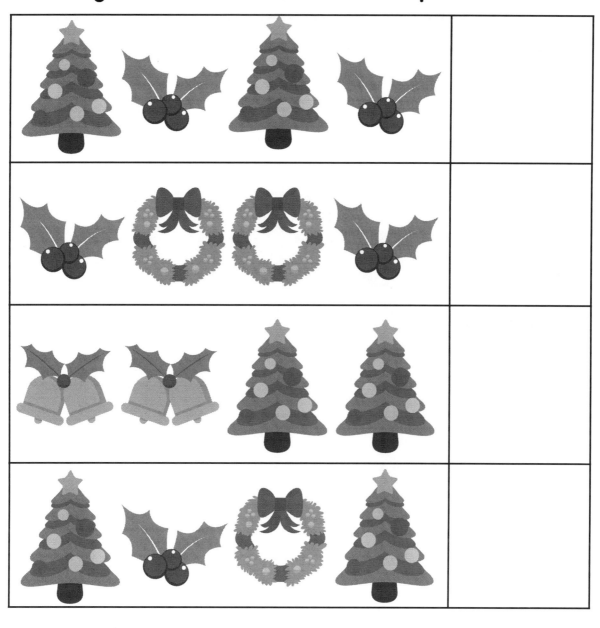

Spell the word

K S E

A T S

☐ ☐ ☐ ☐ ☐ ☐

Copy the picture

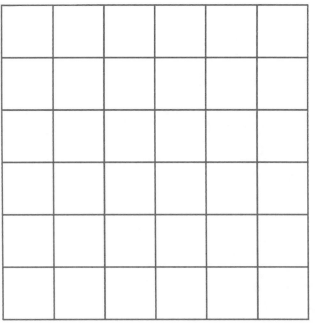

HO! HO! HO!

Thank You For Choosing our Book
Please, don't forget to rate it.

☆ ☆ ☆ ☆ ☆

Dan Harley

Solutions

Page 9

Page 10

Page 12
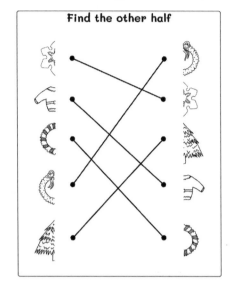

Page 14

Page 17
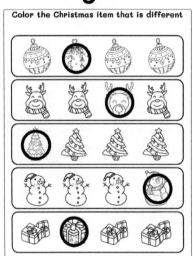

Page 21
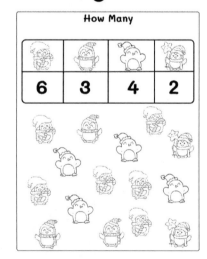

Page 22

Page 23

Page 24

Page 29

SNOWMAN

Page 39

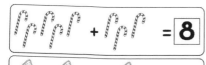

Page 44

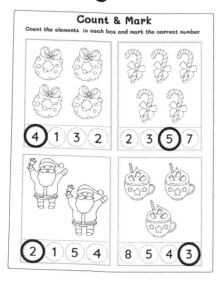

Page 33

COUNTING CATS AND DOGS
Write the answers at the box provided below

CATS 5 7 DOGS

Page 40

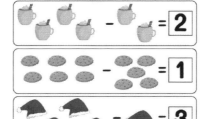

Page 49

Page 34

MATCH THE NUMBER
Draw a line to match the number to its name

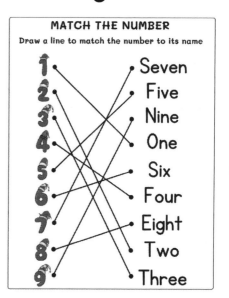

Page 43

SKIP COUNT BY 2'S. FILL IN THE MISSING NUMBERS FOR EACH SWEATER.

Page 50

Page 55

Spot 5 differences and color

Page 56
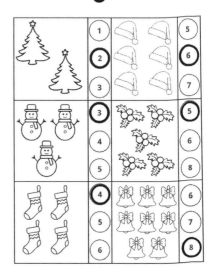

Page 65

Page 66

Find penguin among the snowman

Page 67
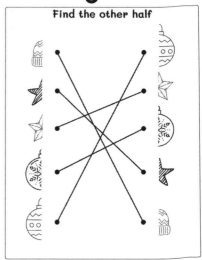
Find the other half

Page 70
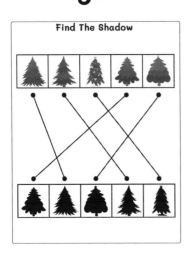
Find The Shadow

Page 75

Page 78
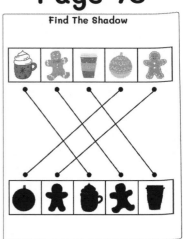
Find The Shadow

Page 80

Page 81
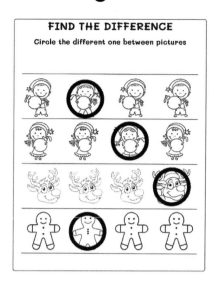

Page 84
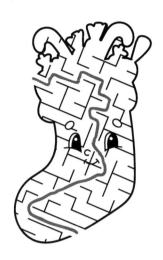

Page 87

SKATES

Made in United States
Orlando, FL
29 November 2023